RICHEL PREVOST

Pacific Coast Highway

The most picturesque road trip you will ever take!

First edition

This book was professionally typeset on Reedsy.
Find out more at reedsy.com

Contents

Introduction

I am so excited to be sharing this book with you. Hello! My name is Richel Prevost. My dad was in the army. Growing up, he was away a lot, so we didn't travel a lot. A typical family holiday was camping, usually close to a lake. We had one BIG family holiday that I'll always remember. This trip was along Interstate 5. It is because of this trip, I was bitten by the travel bug.

This book isn't your typical travel guide. It's more of a planning guide. This book will lead you on a journey from San Diego CA to Bellingham WA, touching on numerous stops that will undoubtedly have the same effect on you,they did on me. Smitten with the most picturesque drive on continental North America.

Although the term Pacific Coast Highway is a term used for only a portion of Interstate 5, for the purpose of this book, I'll refer to the entire stretch as the Pacific Coast Highway. Most of the stops are in California. You'll want to spend extra time in some of the bigger centers, because there's so much to see and do. This book doesn't cover every stop, but highlights some of my personal favorites. Others are stops that I haven't been to yet, but after doing research, I want to visit.

To start with, we'll be traveling from just north of the Mexican border, all the way to just south of the Canadian border. The majority of the stops have beautiful, expansive, sandy beaches. Sandy beaches lend to all the popular activities people enjoy doing at a beach; suntan, picnic, swim, surf, kayak, fish and make sand castles. Because the route is along the Pacific Coastline, almost every stop will provide you with an opportunity to take pictures of not only the breathtaking scenery, but also spectacular sunsets. Something I personally will never tire of.

The best way to get the most out of this book is to highlight all the areas that pique your interest, then pull out your map, and plot your journey. Pack your bags, camera and sunscreen, and enjoy one of the most beautiful drives you'll ever experience.

Southern California

San Diego

You could definitely spend more than a day in San Diego. In fact, there's so much to do that I could dedicate another whole book to San Diego alone. The city is located just 17 miles north of Tijuana, Mexico. Based on its proximity to Mexico, it's safe to say that the weather in San Diego is beautiful, all year round.

Balboa Park

• One of the most popular tourist spots in San Diego is Balboa Park. Set on 1,200 acres, Balboa Park is home to the famous San Diego Zoo, 17 museums (Centro Cultural de la Raza, Museum of Photographic Arts, San Diego Natural History Museum, San Diego History Center, San Diego Air and Space Museum, Fleet Science Center, Forever Balboa Park, San Diego Museum of Art, San Diego Art Institute, Mingei International Museum, Women's Museum of California, San Diego Model Railroad Museum, Veterans Museum and Memorial Center, San Diego Automotive Museum, Old Globe Theater, and and WorldBeat Cultural Center, Timken Museum of Art), the Japanese Friendship Garden and the Botanical Building and Gardens.

San Diego Zoo

- I would feel remiss if I didn't say a little more about the San Diego Zoo. Afterall, it is one of the world's most famous zoos. What makes it so famous? Taking up 100 acres in Balboa Park, the zoo is home to more than 3,700 animals from all around the globe. You'll have a chance to see leopards, jaguars, giraffes, pandas and koalas - just to mention a few. To make your trip to the zoo worthwhile, ensure you've got a minimum of 3 to 4 hours.

La Jolla

- La Jolla is also located within the city of San Diego. Like Balboa Park, you could spend an entire day exploring this area. If you're an outdoor enthusiast you can go golfing, hiking, swimming, surfing, kayaking, cave exploring, check out the tide pools and maybe even see some sea lions. If that's not your cup of tea, there's still plenty to do in La Jolla. Stroll around town to see the amazing murals, visit art galleries, go shopping or have a bite to eat. There's something for everyone to do in La Jolla.

SeaWorld

- A trip to San Diego wouldn't be complete without visiting SeaWorld. SeaWorld is a combination of an amusement park with marine life. You can watch presentations with orca whales, dolphins, sea lions and otters. In-between the presentations, hop onto one of the many rides including: Arctic Rescue (launching spring 2023), Emperor, Manta, Electric Eel, Journey to Atlantis, Shipwreck Rapids, Tidal

Twister, Tentacle Twirl, Aqua Scout, Octarock, Riptide Rescue, Sea Dragon Drop, Sky Tower and the Bayside Skyride.

Carlsbad

- Carlsbad is a great stopping point especially if you have any LEGO fans in your family. LEGOLAND is a combination of theme park, water park and aquarium. This is another attraction that you want to spend some time at. The theme park has 60 rides. You'll find more than 7 waterslides, a Build-A-Raft river, and sandy beaches at the water park. Over 6,000 marine animals make their home in the aquarium.
- If you aren't into LEGO, don't despair, there's still lots to do in Carlsbad. Carlsbad is famous for its long stretch of sandy beach. Carlsbad State Beach is a great place to swim or surf. If you are a lover of flowers, you can visit the 50 acre Flower Fields. The village is host to a variety of restaurants, galleries and shops. In fact, Carlsbad has a shopping outlet with over 90 stores including high end fashion brands, like: Gucci, Prada and Michael Kors.

Los Angeles

The second largest metropolis in the USA, Los Angeles is home to many must see attractions.

Hollywood Walk of Fame / TCL Theater

- The Hollywood Walk of Fame is a sidewalk along Hollywood Boulevard that pays tribute to over 2,700 stars (about 20 new stars, from 6 different categories are added each year). Imprints of hands, feet and signatures can be found of some of the greatest

Hollywood legends, at the TCL Chinese Theater (formerly known as Grauman's Chinese Theater). The theater is also located on Hollywood Boulevard. If I had to choose either the Walk of Fame or the TCL Theater, I would choose TCL - hands down. Literally. Hands down in the cement to see how I measure up to some of the greatest legends.

Rodeo Drive

- Rodeo Drive is a famous shopping district known for its high end fashion boutiques and fine dining. Don't be surprised if you spot a celebrity while you're strolling along Rodeo Drive. Whether or not you can afford to shop at Rodeo Drive, it's still fun to have a look around.

Disneyland

- One of the most famous, if not the most famous theme parks in the world, is Disneyland. Whether you're 1 or 100, there is magic inside those walls. Across from Disneyland is the Disney California Adventure Park. Both are worth a visit. Home to all our favorite Disney characters and a total of 67 attractions (this includes rides), you'll be busy all day long.

Universal Studios

- Universal Studios will give you a peak behind the scenes as to how some movies are made, via a trolley tour of the studio. There are rides and attractions spanning many genres of movies. Some of the attractions include: Jaws, Jurassic Park, the Fast and Furious and Harry Potter.

Huntington Beach

- If you're a surfing enthusiast, you've got to make a stop in Huntington Beach. Home to the International Surf Museum, and dubbed Surf City USA, Huntington Beach has something for new and experienced surfers alike.The nickname Surf City USA came about, because it has some of the best surf conditions in California.
- Besides great surfing, Huntington Beach has one of the longest piers. The pier is a great place to fish or simply people watch.If you brought your bicycle along, you can ride along the 10 mile stretch of paved trail. A great way to take in the whole beach area.

Santa Monica Beach

- At 3.5 miles of sandy beach, and the location where Baywatch was filmed, Santa Monica is a popular area to take a stroll, play beach volleyball, swim or surf.
- The town itself is only 8.5 miles, so it's possible to tour the streets in a day, taking in shopping, restaurants and museums. One of the most appealing areas to shop is the Third Street Promenade, which is a pedestrian only shopping area. Santa Monica Pier is home to shops, restaurants, an amusement park, arcade and aquarium.
- Home to the original Muscle Beach, which was established during the depression, you can still find retro equipment like parallel bars, ropes and swings. The equipment is free to use, so if you're a fitness buff and not shy about an audience, this is a beautiful backdrop for a workout. If you're feeling adventurous, you can even take part in the trapeze school.

Venice Beach

- Only 3 miles north of Santa Monica, is Venice Beach. If you are into people watching,the Venice Beach boardwalk is a must. Eclectic or eccentric, you decide. Tattoo shops and souvenir shops are the backdrop for fortune tellers, buskers, musicians and skaters (board and roller). The Roller Skate Dance Plaza and the Venice Skate Park are sure to provide you with hours of entertainment. What would a stop at Venice Beach be, without checking out Muscle Beach? Not to be confused with the Santa Monica Muscle Beach, there is a fee to work out at Venice Beach.If you plan accordingly, you might be able to take in a world class bodybuilding competition.

Malibu

- Having famous actors or musicians living in the area, it's not uncommon for tourists to experience a celebrity sighting. Besides living in the area, Malibu is also home to many famous restaurants and private clubs that these celebrities frequent.
- Three beaches lay within the Malibu area; Surfrider, Zuma and Point Dume State beaches.
- Not to be outdone by the three beaches, there are three great hiking trails in Malibu: Escondido Falls Trail, Solstice Canyon Trail and the Malibu Creek State Park.
- If you just want to kick back, listen to some great live music and do some wine tasting, Malibu Wines is the most popular winery in the area.

SOUTHERN CALIFORNIA

Central California

Santa Barbara

Butterfly Beach

- Tired of beautiful beaches? I didn't think so. Santa Barbara has their fair share including; East Beach, West Beach and Butterfly Beach.
- Between East and West Beach, you'll find Stearns Wharf. The pier has shops, restaurants and a museum.
- As for Butterfly Beach, it gets its name from the migratory Monarch butterflies that make the eucalyptus plants, around the beach, their home during winter months. If you love butterflies, as much as I do, it's a great opportunity to take photos of something other than the beautiful coastal views and stunning sunsets.

Seven Falls Trail

- Although not a leisurely stroll, the hike up the Seven Falls Trail is well worth it. A 3.5 mile (return) trek will take you through canyons and creek crossings. When you reach the top, you'll have an incredible view of the falls. If you need to cool off after your hike, you can jump into the cool waters at the base of the falls. Butterflies and rainbows, Santa Barbara has it.

Santa Barbara Zoo

- If you didn't get an opportunity to stop at the San Diego Zoo, you've got a second chance in Santa Barbara. The Santa Barbara Zoo is not as big as the San Diego Zoo, but it still has about 500 animals, so it's worth a visit. Lions and giraffes, if you want to see them, the Santa Barbara Zoo has you covered.
- Are you a history buff? If so, I'd recommend visiting the Santa Barbara Mission. Even though it's still an active parish, they welcome thousands of visitors year round. The mission is one of the best preserved of the 21 California missions. Architecture, religious artifacts and beautiful gardens are sure to please everyone, not just the history buff.

Solvang

- Solvang is Danish for 'sunny field'. A quaint Danish-style city, Solvang will likely remind you of Denmark with its European architecture, including thatched rooftops and windmills.
- The Elverhoj Museum showcases the history and culture of Solvang. The Elverhoj Museum isn't the only museum in Solvang. You can also visit the Hans Christian Andersen Museum. Hans Christian Andersen is a famous Danish author who penned classic fairy tales like, 'The Emperor's New Clothes', 'The Princess and the Pea', 'The Ugly Duckling' and 'The Little Mermaid'.
- A trip to Solvang just wouldn't be complete without partaking in Danish pastries. Three of the more popular bakeries in Solvang are Birkholm's Bakery and Cafe, Olsen's Danish Village Bakery and

Mortensen's Bakery. They are busy spots, but well worth the wait.

Pismo Beach

- Pismo Beach is home to another Monarch Butterfly natural habitat. Thousands of butterflies make their way to the Monarch Butterfly Grove annually. Their migration is during the winter months (October to February), and is truly a magnificent sight.
- Pismo Beach is also famous for their sand dunes. You can access the dunes by ATV, horseback or even by foot. The dunes are considered some of the largest in California and stretch for 5 miles.

Morro Bay

- If you don't mind cold water, Morro Bay will wake you up if you want to jump in for a swim. If you'd rather stay warm, there's plenty of golden sand to tan on.
- During the winter months, the waves get quite a bit larger than in summer. I wouldn't recommend surfing the waves during this time, unless you're an experienced surfer.
- There's plenty of fishing opportunities available in the bay too. You can fish from the beach, or rent a boat and go out into the bay.
- For something a little more different, ensure you bring your binoculars, so that you can bird watch. Morro Bay is home to several different species of birds including cormorants and pelicans.

Big Sur

- Big Sur is a region that will surely provide you with jaw dropping scenery. There are several state parks along the way giving you breathtaking views of the coastline and the redwood forest. Three of the parks include; Pfeiffer Big Sur State Park, Andrew Molera State Park and Julia Pfeiffer Burns State Park.

- You won't want to bypass Pfeiffer Big Sur State Park, home of Pfieffer Beach. Pfieffer Beach has pockets of purple sand, mostly visible after a rainfall or close to the tide pools. There is also a keyhole arch at Pfieffer Beach. If timed right, you can capture a picture with the sunlight pouring through the keyhole, which sometimes resembles fire.
- Another photo opp you won't want to miss is the Bixby Creek Bridge (featured on the cover of this book). Due to the design and setting of the bridge, it's considered one of California's most photographed bridges.

Carmel by the Sea

- Carmel-by-the-Sea (or Carmel), is an art enthusiast's dream. Some galleries feature local artists, while others feature international artists. Home to over 100 art galleries, there's something for every art lover.
- Carmel is also home to Carmel Beach. It's a stunning, white-sand beach with panoramic views of Pebble Beach and Point Lobos. It's the perfect spot for sunbathing, swimming, surfing and kayaking.
- If you missed the Santa Barbara Mission, here's another opportunity for you to visit a historic mission. The Carmel Mission (aka Mission San Carlos Borromeo del Rio Carmelo), is one of California's more historic missions. The mission offers guided tours of their grounds.

Monterey

- Monterey Bay Aquarium is a popular stop. Home to 35,000 fish and marine animals from around the globe.
- If you'd rather see sea life in their natural habitat, Monterey is a great location to go whale watching. Different species of whales inhabit the waters off of Monterey at different times of the year. If you're interested in seeing a Sperm, Orca or Gray whale, the best time to go whale watching is between December through May. From May to November, you're more likely to see a Humpback or Blue whale.
- If it's a dolphin you want to catch a glimpse of, you're in luck no matter what time of year you visit. Besides dolphins you may catch sight of sea lions, sea otters and seals.
- You can book a whale watching tour at the 'Old Fisherman's Wharf'. The historic wharf has been around since the 1800s. Visit a restaurant in the wharf for some of the freshest seafood you've ever tasted.

Santa Cruz

Natural Bridges State Park

- If you still haven't had your fill of beautiful beaches, you should check out Natural Bridges State Beach. When the tide is low, tide pools are exposed. This is a great opportunity to explore and see all kinds of marine wildlife like: starfish, anemones and crabs. Also visible at low tide is the beach's namesake, a natural bridge rock formation that spans the cove. You can suntan, swim, picnic and even head out for a hike at this beach.

Seymour Marine Discovery Center

- If you're interested in learning more about marine mammals, birds, fish and the ecosystem in the area, the Seymour Marine Discovery Center is a great place to check out. The Center provides visitors with an opportunity to visit their touch tank. There is even a deep sea tank with a realistic model of a giant squid. You can take a walk through the center on your own, or take part in a guided tour. If you're really hungry for information, you can even listen to a lecture given by a marine scientist.

UCSC Arboretum

- At the UCSC Arboretum you'll be able to explore 135 acres of beautiful gardens, with plants from all over the world. There are hiking trails for visitors, taking you from region to region. There's a succulent garden, a New Zealand garden, a South African garden, a Mediterranean garden, and of course a California garden. If you would rather, you can participate in a guided tour, a workshop or even one of their classes.

Northern California

Half Moon Bay

Mavericks Surf Spot

- Mavericks is a world famous spot for experienced surfers. The waves can reach a height of 60 feet, the water is cold and the currents are strong. Unless you are an expert surfer, you'd do better to watch from the sandy beach… but what a show.

Coastal Trail

- Just as its name suggests, the trail runs along the coastline. The Coastal Trail is accessible to hikers and bikers alike. If you didn't bring your bike along, there are several locations in Half Moon Bay where you can rent one. You don't want to hike or bike? How about a horseback ride? Take a guided horseback ride along the trail with Sea Horse Ranch. Ensure that you book ahead.

San Francisco

When I think of San Francisco, I think of rows of Victorian Houses, trolley cars and hills. Lots of hills. It is a beautiful city with some noteworthy landmarks.

Golden Gate Bridge

- The Golden Gate Bridge is one of the world's most recognizable bridges. As a suspension bridge 1.7 miles long, it is considered the world's longest suspension bridge. You can drive across it, take a bus, rent a bike or even walk the bridge. It is an iconic stop that you won't want to miss.

Alcatraz

- Alcatraz, a small island off San Francisco, was home to one of the most famous prisons in America. The prison housed many of the most notorious criminals in history. Closed in 1963, it is now open for tours to the public. It is said that the prison is haunted by many of the spirits. You can visit the cells, the recreation yard and dining hall, just to name a few areas. An interesting piece of history that is worth taking some time out to see.

Fisherman's Wharf

- San Francisco's Fisherman's Wharf is one of the most popular wharfs in North America. Home to many restaurants, giving you an opportunity to dine on fresh seafood from the area. Clam chowder served in a bread bowl is one of the area's most famous dishes. Not into clams? Try the Dungeness crab or shrimp. So delicious!

Lombard Street

- There are certain sites that are worth visiting, even for the opportunity to simply say you've visited. Lombard Street is one that you don't want to miss. Although not official, it is considered by locals as the crookedest street in the world. It's only a quarter of a mile long, but in that short span has 8 hairpin turns and is on a hill. Not for the faint of heart.

ChinaTown

- San Francisco's ChinaTown is the largest in North America. It spans 24 full city blocks and is home to many souvenir shops, gift shops, boutiques and restaurants. If you want to spend some time immersing yourself in Chinese culture, this is the place for you.

Point Reyes National Seashore

- Point Reyes is 71,000 acres of protected area. Beautiful rugged shoreline, spectacular views with 150 miles of hiking trails, makes it a great stopping point for the outdoor enthusiast.
- There are 490 species of birds in the area. If you're a bird watcher, make sure you bring your binoculars with you.
- Interested in the history and culture of the Indigenous people of the area? There are a smattering of buildings and cultural sites that will give you insight into the history of the region.
- Don't forget to stop at the Point Reyes Lighthouse. The lighthouse is open to the public, but is only open certain days during the week and can close due to inclement weather. Be sure you check ahead of time to ensure it's open during the time you plan to visit. Don't forget to wear a good pair of shoes. There are 308 stairs leading

down to the lighthouse. If you go down, you've got to go back up.

Bodega Bay

- Bodega Bay's harbor is home to a large fleet of commercial fishing boats. Seafood you can expect in this area includes: oysters, salmon and crab.
- A popular spot for kayaking, hiking and birdwatching, the Bodega Bay area is stunning. Speaking of birds... if you've seen the Alfred Hichcock movie, 'The Birds', you might recognize some of the landmarks from the movie. The Birds was filmed in Bodega Bay.

Mendocino

- Looking for something a little different to do? Why not take a tour of the Anderson Valley Brewing Company. Visit the tasting room where you can sample the award winning beer. There's a shop where you can purchase some brew or take home some souvenir glasses.
- Beer isn't the only beverage made in Mendocino. Mendocino is home to 24 wine tasting rooms. Some of the best chardonnay and pinot noir grapes are grown in the area. If they are one of your favorites, you'll want to check out one of the many wineries.

Avenue of the Giants

- The Avenue of the Giants isn't on the Pacific Coast Highway, but it's something you are going to want to see, as long as you don't mind a little detour. About 20 miles south of the town of Leggett (off highway 101), is where you'll find this spectacular span of Redwood trees. Redwoods are some of the largest and oldest trees in the world, living to be about 2000 years old. The Redwood can reach heights of 300-350 ft tall and a diameter of about 30 ft around. Nature at her finest.

Trinidad

- Trinidad is a beautiful coastal town that provides visitors an opportunity to enjoy swimming, surfing and exploring the tide pools.
- Trinidad Head is a hike easy enough for any skill level of hiker and provides stunning panoramic views of the coastline.
- In town, you can visit the museum or the art gallery.
- Just north of the town is Moonstone Beach. Popular for its white sand and abundance of moonstones.

Redwoods National and State Parks

- Just like the Avenue of the Giants, the Redwoods National and State Parks aren't directly on the Pacific Coast Highway. You'll find the parks only 50 miles east of the Pacific Coast Highway. There are lots of hiking trails which lend to a variety of wildlife sightings. If you aren't comfortable hiking on your own, you can take a ranger-led hike. Camping, fishing are also popular activities in this region.

Crescent City

- Just 20 miles south of Oregon, our last stop in California is Crescent City. Home to South Beach, Pebble Beach and St. George Beach, there's no shortage of places to swim, surf or suntan.
- If you want to take in views of the area, you can visit the Battery Point Lighthouse.

- Oceanworld Aquarium is in Crescent City and gives visitors an opportunity to see a variety of marine wildlife including sharks, seals and sea lions. If you're feeling adventurous, you can even swim with the sea lions.

Oregon

Gold Beach

- Gold Beach is a beautiful sandy beach that stretches for miles.
- There are a few attractions in the area that are unique. The Prehistoric Gardens is a botanical garden, sitting on approximately 2 acres. Throughout the garden you will find 20 life size dinosaur replicas, including: the ever popular Tyrannosaurus Rex, Triceratops and Stegosaurus.
- If dinosaurs aren't of interest to you, what about golf? There's a 9 hole golf course right on the beach. (I can only imagine how tricky those sand traps are.)

Bandon

- Bandon Marsh National Wildlife Refuge is a great place to observe different species of wildlife and birds. You may even see a bald eagle.
- Bandon is home to several world class golf courses, including the Bandon Dunes Golf Resort, which has been ranked as one of the world's finest.
- Face Rock State Scenic Viewpoint is a great lookout location for

amazing views of the coastline and the famous Face Rock formation. Legend says that the formation is the petrified face of a young girl who was told by her elders to stay away from the waters. The ocean current pulled her out to sea and the gods punished her by petrifying her as a warning to others of the dangers of the ocean and not listening to your elders.

Coos Bay

- Shore Acres Park is a beautiful mix of lush gardens, hiking trails, picnic areas and incredible scenic views of the ocean.
- If you're interested in local history, including Native American, you can visit the Coos History Museum. Coos Bay is also a popular crabbing location. In fact, if you're interested, you can take a guided tour.
- After your tour, why not partake in some of the local cuisine. Besides crab, halibut and salmon are popular fish caught in the area.

Newport

- Not to be outdone by other coastal towns, Newport has an aquarium. Not just any aquarium, but an award winning aquarium. The Oregon Coast Aquarium has won several awards, including the Traveller's Choice Award.
- Devil's Punchbowl State Natural area is a unique setting. It's a cove formed in the shape of a punchbowl, the area is a great place to explore and hike.
- If you're in the area between December and the beginning of January, or March to the beginning of April, you might catch a glimpse of migrating gray whales.

Lincoln City

- Feeling lucky in Lincoln City? You can visit the Chinook Winds Casino Resort. Besides gambling, the casino offers live entertainment and fine dining.
- If you're interested in tax-free shopping on name-brand merchandise, you won't want to miss out on the Lincoln City Outlets.
- Depending on the time of year that you visit Lincoln City, you may be able to take in one of the festivals they host annually. The Kite Festival, Summer Folk Festival and Chowder and Brew Festivals are three you might want to check out.
- If you want to enjoy nature, don't despair, there are plenty of beaches and hiking trails for you to enjoy.

Depoe Bay

- You will have an opportunity, depending upon the time of year you're visiting, to see gray whales along the Oregon coast. However, Depoe Bay is one of the best places in the world to watch them from land. There is a Whale Watching Centre, and you can even book a whale watching tour.
- Besides gray whales, one of the top attractions in Depoe Bay is the Spouting Horn. The Spouting Horn is a hole formed in the rocks. When the waves crash into the rocks, the water spouts up from the formation, like a whale's blowhole.

Tillamook

- If you're a history buff, you're going to love the Tillamook Air Museum. Besides the vintage aircraft, Tillamook Air Museum is home to a WWII Blimp hangar.

- Cheese lovers are going to love Tillamook. Tillamook Creamery not only offers cheese tastings and tours, but also has a museum that tells of the history of dairy in Oregon.
- Blue Heron French Cheese Company is a gourmet style food store that offers not only cheese but also wine to pair with it.

Cannon Beach

- Haystack Rock is located in Cannon Beach. It's a 235 foot sea stack that's inhabited by a variety of marine life and birds. A couple of species of wildlife you may see are the tufted puffin or the harbor seal.
- The Cannon Beach History Center and Museum is a great place to learn more about the local history, including Native American tribes. There are interactive displays, photographs and artifacts.

Seaside

- Seaside has a promenade that runs parallel to the beach and stretches 1.5 miles. It's a great place to go for a walk or people watch.
- The Seaside Aquarium is relatively small, but fascinating all the same. One of the exhibits is home to an octopus.
- Depending on when you visit Seaside, you may be able to take part in one of their many festivals or activities. You can check out the Beach Volleyball Tournament, the Seaside First Saturday Art Walk or the Seaside Aquarium Crab Feed.

Astoria

- The 125 foot tall tower, Astoria Column, will provide you with a great vantage point of the ocean and Columbia River.
- The Riverwalk is a walkway that runs alongside the Columbia River. It's a great place to take a stroll, people watch and even visit local shops along the way.
- The Oregon Film Museum features movies made in Oregon. Astoria's claim to fame includes the movie 'The Goonies', which was filmed in Astoria in 1985.
- During the winter of 1805-1806, explorers Lewis and Clark stayed in an area just outside Astoria called Fort Clatsop National Historic Park. Currently there is a replica fort you can explore and learn about the historic expedition.

Washington

Long Beach

- Discovery Trail is located in Long Beach. It's an almost 8 mile long, paved walkway along the beach.
- The World Kite Museum is dedicated to the history and art of kites. The museum is a great place to learn about different types of kites, and to see some amazing displays.
- If you missed visiting Fort Clatsop in Astoria, you have another opportunity to learn about Lewis and Clark, at the Lewis and Clark Interpretive Center.

Ocean Shores

- Ocean Shores is famous for its long stretches of sandy beaches, with lots of opportunity for both beach and water activities.
- Several festivals and events are held throughout the year at Ocean Shores. If you're there at the right time, you might be able to participate in the sand castle competitions, kite flying festival or check out a car show.
- Museums, galleries and shopping are all available in Ocean Shores.
- If you're a golf enthusiast, there are 3 golf courses in the vicinity.

Westport

- Westport has miles of sandy beaches, conducive to both water and beach activities. Have you ever been kiteboarding? Perhaps Westport would be a great place to try it out. Westport has the best kiteboarding conditions in the Pacific Northwest.
- Fishing is abundant in Westport. You can even charter a boat and go deep-sea fishing.
- Westport Lighthouse or Grays Harbor Lighthouse, you can visit them both. If you want to visit the tallest lighthouse on the Pacific west coast, then go to Grays Harbor. Climb to the top for spectacular views.
- You can visit the Cranberry Museum and learn about the cranberry industry.
- Westport Winery is a great place to taste test local wines. There's also a restaurant onsite. After your meal, you can take a stroll and enjoy the gardens.

Olympic National Park

- Mount Olympus is in Olympic National Park (not to be confused with the Greek God Zuess's home in Greece). It is the highest peak in the park and offers stunning views. If you're an experienced hiker or climber, Mount Olympus will provide you with some challenging vertical climbs.
- There are only 4 rainforests located in the U.S. Two are located in Alaska, one is in Puerto Rico and the fourth is in Olympic National Park. The Hoh Rainforest is on the western side of the park and offers a variety of lush vegetation including ferns and moss.
- Sol Duc Valley is home to the Sol Duc River, which in turn is part of the Sol Duc Falls. After a busy day of hiking and exploring, you

can take a dip in the mineral-rich hot springs.

- Hurricane Ridge is located on the north side of the park. Stunning views of the park, including Mount Olympus can be seen from Hurricane Ridge. It's a great place to hike and view wildlife.

Tacoma

- The museum district is home to three recommended stops. First is the Tacoma Art Museum. Here you will find exhibits from not only artists from all over America, but also regional artists. The Washington State History Museum will give you insight into the area's history and culture. For the glass-blowing enthusiast, you'll want to visit the Museum of Glass. Here you'll be able to take in some incredible glass exhibits, along with an opportunity to watch glass-blowing demonstrations.
- Across from the Museum of Glass is a pedestrian bridge called the Chihuly Bridge. The bridge is named after renowned glass artist Dale Chihuly. A stunning display of glass unlike anything you've seen before.
- Tacoma Glass Blowing Studio is a great place to visit if you'd like to try the art form out for yourself. Under direct guidance of skilled glass blowers, you can try your hand at creating your own glass piece.
- It has been a little while since we visited an aquarium and zoo in the same city. You can do so in Tacoma at the Point Defiance Park. If you'd like to stop and smell the roses, you can do so at the Point Defiance Rose Garden.
- If you are an antique car enthusiast, you'll want to stop at LeMay - America's Car Museum. Rare and vintage cars, numbering over 1,500 can be found in the museum. It's an impressive collection of cars and includes some that date back as far as the 1800s.

Seattle

- The Space Needle is probably the most iconic landmark in Seattle. The Space Needle was one of the locations used to shoot the movie 'Sleepless in Seattle'. It's also seen in quite a few episodes of Grey's Anatomy. From the top of the tower, you get a panoramic view of the area. You can even dine in the rotating restaurant found at the top of the Space Needle.
- Pike Place Market is well known for the famous flying fish. When orders for fish are placed, the fishmongers yell out to one another and toss the fish from fishmonger to fishmonger. It's an entertaining way to purchase your fish. The market has plenty more than just fish. It is also well known for their fresh produce and craft vendors.
- The Seattle waterfront is a great place to take a stroll and enjoy the views of Elliot Bay. You can visit the Seattle Aquarium along the waterfront, or take a ride on the Seattle Great Wheel. The Seattle Great Wheel is a large ferris wheel that will give you stunning views of the city's skyline.
- Also found along the waterfront is the Olympic Sculpture Park. You can enjoy the beauty of Puget Sound and the Olympic Mountains, while taking in the collection of outdoor sculptures.

Bellingham

- Our last stop on our journey is Bellingham. You'll want to visit the Fairhaven Historic District. A charming area filled with 19th century architecture, galleries, shops and cafes.
- Away from the bustle of the city, you'll find Whatcom Falls Park. Hiking the trails that take you through the lush forest you'll cross the Grand Stone Bridge. Built around 1940, it is as magical as its

surroundings. From the bridge you'll have a beautiful view of the Whatcom Falls.

Conclusion

My hope is that you've enjoyed this journey along the Pacific Coast Highway with me. Hopefully you were able to find some areas that are of interest to you, where you'd like to visit. Some familiar, some new. Even though we drove the highway when I was younger, I didn't have the opportunity to visit every stop mentioned in this book. It has certainly stirred up a lot of great memories, and reignited my passion for this particular road trip. Who knows, perhaps one day we'll run into each other at one of the stops.

If you found this book helpful, I would be appreciative if you'd leave a favorable review for the book on Amazon.

References

Avenue of the Giants. (n.d.). https://www.visitredwoods.com/explore-t he-redwoods/avenue-of-the-giants/

Awesome Awaits at LEGOLAND® Parks and Hotels. (n.d.). LEGOLAND. https://www.legoland.com/

Booker, C. (2023, March 31). 23 Best Things to Do in Tacoma, Washington (in 2023) - Travel Lemming - Travel Lemming. *Travel Lemming*. https://travellemming.com/things-to-do-in-tacoma/

Brown, A. (2021). 8 Top Things to Do in Bandon, Oregon. *TripSavvy*. https://www.tripsavvy.com/fun-things-to-do-in-bandon-1608493

Cannon Beach Things to Do | Shopping, Hiking & Haystack Rock. (n.d.). https://www.cannonbeach.org/things-to-do/

Carmel-By-The-Sea, C. (n.d.). *Carmel-by-the-Sea, California Official Travel Site*. Carmel-by-the-Sea, California. https://www.carmelcalifor nia.com/

City of Monterey, CA. (n.d.). https://monterey.org/

Del Norte County, V. (2022, November 8). *Official Visitor Guide to Crescent City, California- Visit Del Norte County*. Visit Crescent City & Del Norte County California. https://visitdelnortecounty.com/article/ crescent-city-travel-guide/

Depoe Bay Activities Archives - Channel House. (n.d.). Channel House. https://www.channelhouse.com/our-blog/category/depoe-bay-activit ies/

Experience Westport, Washington. (2023, March 29). Experience Westport, Washington. https://www.experiencewestport.com/welcome?gclid=Cj0KCQjw9deiBhC1ARIsAHLjR2DE0NRw7x3YzGO2L4v__AOxKZZiFYNEaCAtTVCl7kM_412nKvxHF_AaAubQEALw_wcB

Gold Beach Oregon. (n.d.). *Recreation | Gold Beach Oregon.* https://goldbeachoregon.com/recreation/

Home | Venice Beach | City of Los Angeles Department of Recreation and Parks. (n.d.). https://www.laparks.org/venice/

Home - Morro Bay, CA - Official Visitor Guide. (n.d.). https://www.morrobay.org/

Johnson, J. (2022, July 15). 18 HIDDEN GEMS IN LA JOLLA | Hidden San Diego. *Hidden San Diego.* https://hiddensandiego.com/hidden-gems-of-la-jolla.php

Keller, E. (2023). The 21 Best Things To Do In Trinidad, California (2023). *Discovering Hidden Gems.* https://discoveringhiddengems.com/things-to-do-in-trinidad-california/

Long Beach Peninsula. (n.d.). Visit the USA. https://www.visittheusa.ca/destination/long-beach-peninsula

Malibu | Visit California. (n.d.). https://www.visitcalifornia.com/places-to-visit/malibu/

McFadden, M. (2022). 31 Things to do in Mendocino, California for the Perfect Weekend Away. *The Atlas Heart.* https://theatlasheart.com/things-to-do-in-mendocino/

Newport, OR Attractions | Home to Oregon's Tallest Lighthouse. (2021, October 21). Travel Oregon. https://traveloregon.com/places-to-go/cities/newport/

Official Visitor Guide for Solvang in the Santa Ynez Valley -Solvang, California. (n.d.). https://www.solvangusa.com/

Oregon Coast Visitors Center. (2021, February 8). *Coos Bay - Oregon Coast Visitors Association.* Oregon Coast Visitors Association. https://visittheoregoncoast.com/cities/coos-bay/

Reshma. (2022, April 19). *35 Amazing Things To Do In Point Reyes California.* The Solo Globetrotter | Solo Female Travel Blog. https://th esologlobetrotter.com/things-to-do-in-point-reyes/

Russell, B. S. I. S. (n.d.). *Big Sur Beach Guide, Big Sur California.* https://www.bigsurcalifornia.org/beaches.html

Santa Barbara, CA | Hotels, Restaurants, Events & Activities. (2023, May 1). Visit Santa Barbara. https://santabarbaraca.com/

SANTA CRUZ BEACH BOARDWALK. (2019, October 1). Visit California. https://www.visitcalifornia.com/in/attraction/santa-cr uz-beach-boardwalk?gclid=Cj0KCQjw9deiBhC1ARIsAHLjR2BxPTBe QfnsR7f9XFlm55b6hTwLeJU7lWux7h1j3bPFimJ4AvXseYwaAuBYE ALw_wcB

Santa Monica Travel & Tourism. (2023). Homepage. *Visit Santa Monica.* https://www.santamonica.com/

Sarouhan, T. (2021, April 28). Get to Know Historic Balboa Park's Past. *https://www.govisitsandiego.com/things-to-do/history/history-of-balb oa-park/.* Retrieved May 6, 2023, from https://www.govisitsandiego.co m/things-to-do/history/history-of-balboa-park/

Schultz, A. (n.d.). *12 Best Things to Do in Lincoln City, Oregon.* Touropia. https://www.touropia.com/things-to-do-in-lincoln-city-oregon/

Search Results. (n.d.). The Official Travel Resource for the San Diego Region. https://www.sandiego.org/search/site.aspx?q=balboa+park

SeaWorld San Diego Theme Park - Aquarium, Zoo & Theme Park in California. (n.d.). https://seaworld.com/san-diego/

TCL Chinese Theatres |. (n.d.). http://www.tclchinesetheatres.com/

Team, T. (2023). 20 Unique Things to do in Seattle, WA. *Travel Makes Me Happy.* https://travelmakesmehappy.com/20-unique-things-to-do- in-seattle-wa/?gclid=Cj0KCQjw9deiBhC1ARIsAHLjR2DZbKwx2PC_ LQeLRfW4a8hYKZ5DUSwCjU75AvAzLAaOchJPiDXkUGoaAgxQEA Lw_wcB#h-best-20-things-to-do-in-seattle

THE TOP 15 Things To Do, Attractions & Activities in San Francisco -

Viator. (n.d.). https://www.viator.com/en-CA/San-Francisco/d651

Tillamook Coast. (2023, January 11). *Tillamook County, Oregon Coast - Beaches, Attractions & Things to Do*. https://tillamookcoast.com/

Top 10 Things To Do In Bellingham. (n.d.). bellingham.org. https://www.bellingham.org/top-10-things-to-do-in-bellingham

Tourism Ocean Shores, Tourism Ocean Shores & Convention Center. (2023, May 1). *Tourism Ocean Shores | Sand & Sawdust Festival 2023*. Tourism Ocean Shores. https://tourismoceanshores.com/

Tripadvisor. (n.d.). *THE 15 BEST Things to Do in Bodega Bay - UPDATED 2023 - Must See Attractions in Bodega Bay, CA | Tripadvisor*. https://www.tripadvisor.ca/Attractions-g32091-Activities-Bodega_Bay_Sonoma_County_California.html

Universal Studios Hollywood - Los Angeles, California - Official Site. (n.d.). Universal Studios Hollywood. https://www.universalstudioshollywood.com/web/en/us

Visit California. (n.d.). https://www.visitcalifornia.com/search/?q=half+moon+bay

Visit Seaside, the Oregon Coast's Favorite Vacation Destination. (n.d.). Seaside Oregon. https://www.seasideor.com/

Visit the Historic Coastal City of Astoria, Oregon. (2021, November 30). Travel Oregon. https://traveloregon.com/places-to-go/cities/astoria/

Walk Of Fame - Hollywood Walk of Fame. (2023, May 4). Hollywood Walk of Fame. https://walkoffame.com/

Wikipedia contributors. (2023a). Balboa Park (San Diego). *Wikipedia*. https://en.wikipedia.org/wiki/Balboa_Park_(San_Diego)

Wikipedia contributors. (2023b). Redwood National and State Parks. *Wikipedia*. https://en.wikipedia.org/wiki/Redwood_National_and_State_Parks

Wildlife. (n.d.). San Diego Zoo. https://zoo.sandiegozoo.org/wildlife

Yogerst, J. (2022, January 25). Everything to know about Olympic National Park. *Travel*. https://www.nationalgeographic.com/travel/na

tional-parks/article/olympic-national-park

Zócalo Public Square. (2009, November 30). *On This Day | Page 3 of 8 | Zócalo Public Square.* https://www.zocalopublicsquare.org/category/o n-this-day/page/3/

Printed in Great Britain
by Amazon

26155377R00030